COPYRIGHT © 2019 Agile Expressions
AgileExpressions.com

Date: _____

Title: _____

The Only
Choice I
Ever Made
Was To Be
Myself

Date:

Title:

The Only
Choice I
Ever Made
Was To Be
Myself

Date: _____

Title: _____

The Only
Choice I
Ever Made
Was To Be
Myself

Date:

Title:

The Only
Choice I
Ever Made
Was To Be
Myself

Date:

Title:

The Only
Choice I
Ever Made
Was To Be
Myself

Date:

Title:

The Only
Choice I
Ever Made
Was To Be
Myself

Date:

Title:

The Only
Choice I
Ever Made
Was To Be
Myself

Date:

Title:

The Only
Choice I
Ever Made
Was To Be
Myself

Date:

Title:

The Only
Choice I
Ever Made
Was To Be
Myself

Date:

Title:

The Only
Choice I
Ever Made
Was To Be
Myself

Date: _____

Title: _____

The Only Choice I Ever Made Was To Be Myself

Date:

Title:

The Only
Choice I
Ever Made
Was To Be
Myself

Date:

Title:

The Only
Choice I
Ever Made
Was To Be
Myself

Date:

Title:

The Only
Choice I
Ever Made
Was To Be
Myself

Date: _____

Title: _____

The Only
Choice I
Ever Made
Was To Be
Myself

Date:

Title:

The Only
Choice I
Ever Made
Was To Be
Myself

Date: _____

Title: _____

The Only
Choice I
Ever Made
Was To Be
Myself

Date:

Title:

The Only
Choice I
Ever Made
Was To Be
Myself

Date:

Title:

The Only
Choice I
Ever Made
Was To Be
Myself

Date:

Title:

The Only
Choice I
Ever Made
Was To Be
Myself

Date: _____

Title: _____

The Only
Choice I
Ever Made
Was To Be
Myself

Date:

Title:

The Only
Choice I
Ever Made
Was To Be
Myself

Date:

Title:

The Only
Choice I
Ever Made
Was To Be
Myself

Date:

Title:

The Only
Choice I
Ever Made
Was To Be
Myself

Date:

Title:

The Only
Choice I
Ever Made
Was To Be
Myself

Date:

Title:

The Only
Choice I
Ever Made
Was To Be
Myself

Date: _____

Title: _____

The Only
Choice I
Ever Made
Was To Be
Myself

Date:

Title:

The Only
Choice I
Ever Made
Was To Be
Myself

Date:

Title:

The Only
Choice J
Ever Made
Was To Be
Myself

Date:

Title:

The Only
Choice I
Ever Made
Was To Be
Myself

Date:

Title:

The Only
Choice I
Ever Made
Was To Be
Myself

Date:

Title:

The Only
Choice I
Ever Made
Was To Be
Myself

Date:

Title:

The Only
Choice I
Ever Made
Was To Be
Myself

Date:

Title:

The Only
Choice I
Ever Made
Was To Be
Myself

Date:

Title:

The Only
Choice I
Ever Made
Was To Be
Myself

Date:

Title:

The Only
Choice I
Ever Made
Was To Be
Myself

Date:

Title:

The Only
Choice I
Ever Made
Was To Be
Myself

Date:

Title:

The Only
Choice I
Ever Made
Was To Be
Myself

Date:

Title:

The Only
Choice I
Ever Made
Was To Be
Myself

Date:

Title:

The Only
Choice I
Ever Made
Was To Be
Myself

Date:

Title:

The Only
Choice I
Ever Made
Was To Be
Myself

Date:

Title:

The Only
Choice I
Ever Made
Was To Be
Myself

Date:

Title:

The Only
Choice I
Ever Made
Was To Be
Myself

Date:

Title:

The Only
Choice I
Ever Made
Was To Be
Myself

Date:

Title:

The Only
Choice I
Ever Made
Was To Be
Myself

Date:

Title:

The Only
Choice I
Ever Made
Was To Be
Myself

Date:

Title:

The Only
Choice I
Ever Made
Was To Be
Myself

Date:

Title:

The Only Choice I Ever Made Was To Be Myself

Date:

Title:

The Only Choice I Ever Made Was To Be Myself

Date:

Title:

The Only
Choice I
Ever Made
Was To Be
Myself

Date:

Title:

The Only
Choice I
Ever Made
Was To Be
Myself

Date:

Title:

The Only
Choice I
Ever Made
Was To Be
Myself

Date:

Title:

The Only
Choice I
Ever Made
Was To Be
Myself

Date:

Title:

The Only
Choice I
Ever Made
Was To Be
Myself

Date:

Title:

The Only
Choice I
Ever Made
Was To Be
Myself

Date:

Title:

The Only
Choice I
Ever Made
Was To Be
Myself

Date:

Title:

The Only
Choice I
Ever Made
Was To Be
Myself

Date:

Title:

The Only
Choice I
Ever Made
Was To Be
Myself

Date:

Title:

The Only
Choice I
Ever Made
Was To Be
Myself

Date:

Title:

The Only
Choice I
Ever Made
Was To Be
Myself

Date:

Title:

The Only
Choice I
Ever Made
Was To Be
Myself

Date:

Title:

The Only
Choice I
Ever Made
Was To Be
Myself

Date:

Title:

The Only
Choice I
Ever Made
Was To Be
Myself

Date:

Title:

The Only
Choice I
Ever Made
Was To Be
Myself

Date:

Title:

The Only
Choice I
Ever Made
Was To Be
Myself

Date:

Title:

The Only
Choice I
Ever Made
Was To Be
Myself

Date:

Title:

The Only
Choice I
Ever Made
Was To Be
Myself

Date:

Title:

The Only
Choice I
Ever Made
Was To Be
Myself

Date:

Title:

The Only
Choice I
Ever Made
Was To Be
Myself

Date:

Title:

The Only
Choice I
Ever Made
Was To Be
Myself

Date: _____

Title: _____

The Only
Choice I
Ever Made
Was To Be
Myself

Date: _____

Title: _____

The Only
Choice I
Ever Made
Was To Be
Myself

Date:

Title:

The Only
Choice I
Ever Made
Was To Be
Myself

Date: _____

Title: _____

The Only
Choice I
Ever Made
Was To Be
Myself

Date:

Title:

Date:

Title:

The Only
Choice I
Ever Made
Was To Be
Myself

Date:

Title:

The Only
Choice I
Ever Made
Was To Be
Myself

Date:

Title:

The Only
Choice I
Ever Made
Was To Be
Myself

Date:

Title:

The Only
Choice I
Ever Made
Was To Be
Myself

Date:

Title:

The Only
Choice I
Ever Made
Was To Be
Myself

Date:

Title:

The Only
Choice I
Ever Made
Was To Be
Myself

Date:

Title:

The Only
Choice I
Ever Made
Was To Be
Myself

Date:

Title:

The Only
Choice I
Ever Made
Was To Be
Myself

Date:

Title:

The Only
Choice I
Ever Made
Was To Be
Myself

Date:

Title:

The Only
Choice I
Ever Made
Was To Be
Myself

Date:

Title:

The Only
Choice I
Ever Made
Was To Be
Myself

Date:

Title:

The Only
Choice I
Ever Made
Was To Be
Myself

Date:

Title:

The Only
Choice I
Ever Made
Was To Be
Myself

Date:

Title:

The Only
Choice I
Ever Made
Was To Be
Myself

Date:

Title:

The Only
Choice I
Ever Made
Was To Be
Myself

Date:

Title:

The Only
Choice I
Ever Made
Was To Be
Myself

Date:

Title:

The Only
Choice I
Ever Made
Was To Be
Myself

Date:

Title:

The Only
Choice I
Ever Made
Was To Be
Myself

Date:

Title:

The Only
Choice I
Ever Made
Was To Be
Myself

Date:

Title:

The Only
Choice I
Ever Made
Was To Be
Myself

Date:

Title:

The Only
Choice I
Ever Made
Was To Be
Myself

Date:

Title:

The Only
Choice I
Ever Made
Was To Be
Myself

Date:

Title:

The Only
Choice I
Ever Made
Was To Be
Myself

Date:

Title:

The Only
Choice I
Ever Made
Was To Be
Myself

Date:

Title:

The Only
Choice I
Ever Made
Was To Be
Myself

Date:

Title:

The Only
Choice I
Ever Made
Was To Be
Myself

Date:

Title:

The Only
Choice I
Ever Made
Was To Be
Myself

Date:

Title:

The Only
Choice I
Ever Made
Was To Be
Myself

Date:

Title:

The Only
Choice I
Ever Made
Was To Be
Myself

Date:

Title:

The Only
Choice I
Ever Made
Was To Be
Myself

Date:

Title:

The Only
Choice I
Ever Made
Was To Be
Myself

Date: _____

Title: _____

The Only
Choice I
Ever Made
Was To Be
Myself

Date:

Title:

The Only
Choice I
Ever Made
Was To Be
Myself

Date:

Title:

The Only
Choice I
Ever Made
Was To Be
Myself

Date:

Title:

The Only
Choice I
Ever Made
Was To Be
Myself

Date:

Title:

The Only
Choice I
Ever Made
Was To Be
Myself

Date:

Title:

The Only
Choice I
Ever Made
Was To Be
Myself

Date:

Title:

The Only
Choice I
Ever Made
Was To Be
Myself

Date:

Title:

The Only
Choice I
Ever Made
Was To Be
Myself

Date:

Title:

The Only
Choice I
Ever Made
Was To Be
Myself

Date:

Title:

The Only
Choice I
Ever Made
Was To Be
Myself

Date:

Title:

The Only
Choice I
Ever Made
Was To Be
Myself

Date:

Title:

The Only
Choice I
Ever Made
Was To Be
Myself

Date:

Title:

The Only
Choice I
Ever Made
Was To Be
Myself

Date:

Title:

The Only
Choice I
Ever Made
Was To Be
Myself

Date:

Title:

The Only
Choice I
Ever Made
Was To Be
Myself

Date:

Title:

The Only
Choice I
Ever Made
Was To Be
Myself

Date:

Title:

Date:

Title:

The Only
Choice I
Ever Made
Was To Be
Myself

Date:

Title:

The Only
Choice I
Ever Made
Was To Be
Myself

Date:

Title:

The Only
Choice I
Ever Made
Was To Be
Myself

Date:

Title:

The Only
Choice I
Ever Made
Was To Be
Myself

Date:

Title:

The Only
Choice I
Ever Made
Was To Be
Myself

Date:

Title:

The Only
Choice I
Ever Made
Was To Be
Myself

Date:

Title:

The Only
Choice I
Ever Made
Was To Be
Myself

Date:

Title:

The Only
Choice I
Ever Made
Was To Be
Myself

Date:

Title:

The Only
Choice I
Ever Made
Was To Be
Myself

Date:

Title:

The Only
Choice I
Ever Made
Was To Be
Myself

Date:

Title:

The Only
Choice I
Ever Made
Was To Be
Myself

Date:

Title:

The Only
Choice I
Ever Made
Was To Be
Myself

Date:

Title:

The Only
Choice I
Ever Made
Was To Be
Myself

Date:

Title:

The Only
Choice I
Ever Made
Was To Be
Myself

Date:

Title:

The Only
Choice I
Ever Made
Was To Be
Myself

Date:

Title:

The Only
Choice I
Ever Made
Was To Be
Myself

Date:

Title:

The Only
Choice I
Ever Made
Was To Be
Myself

Date:

Title:

The Only
Choice I
Ever Made
Was To Be
Myself

Date:

Title:

The Only
Choice I
Ever Made
Was To Be
Myself

Date:

Title:

The Only
Choice I
Ever Made
Was To Be
Myself

Date:

Title:

The Only
Choice I
Ever Made
Was To Be
Myself

Date:

Title:

The Only
Choice I
Ever Made
Was To Be
Myself

Date:

Title:

The Only
Choice I
Ever Made
Was To Be
Myself

Date:

Title:

The Only
Choice I
Ever Made
Was To Be
Myself

Date:

Title:

The Only
Choice I
Ever Made
Was To Be
Myself

Date: _____

Title: _____

The Only
Choice I
Ever Made
Was To Be
Myself

Date:

Title:

The Only
Choice I
Ever Made
Was To Be
Myself

Made in the
USA
Columbia, SC

80903664R00090